MW00333757

12/79

The Sinking of Clay City

THE SINKING
OF CLAY CITY

Robert Wrigley

COPPER CANYON PRESS   1979

Thanks to the editors of the following publications where some of these poems first appeared: *Big Moon, The Chariton Review, The Chowder Review, The Northwest Review, Poetry Northwest, Scratchgravel Hills, Slackwater Review, Southern Poetry Review, Sou'wester, Stinktree, Wind Literary Journal* and *The Montana Poets Anthology*.

Epigraphs were taken from the following sources:

Neruda and Vallejo: Selected Poems, edited by Robert Bly, translated by Robert Bly, John Knoepfle and James Wright, Beacon Press. Copyright 1971 by Robert Bly.

"Dark as a Dungeon," by Merle Travis. Hill and Range Songs, Inc./Elvis Presley Music, Inc. BMI

In the Outer Dark by Stanley Plumly, Louisiana State University Press. Copyright 1970 by Stanley Plumly.

Angle of Repose by Wallace Stegner, Doubleday. Copyright 1971 by Wallace Stegner.

Thanks to Centrum, Fort Worden State Park, where Copper Canyon is press-in-residence and the National Endowment for the Arts, a federal agency, for a grant which helped make this publication possible.

Copper Canyon Press
Box 271
Port Townsend
Washington 98368

Contents

Migratory Habits

Slides

The Sinking of Clay City

For Vana & Philip

Migratory Habits

Migratory Habits
for my father

Someone called your hair *salt and pepper*.
You laughed: more like sparrow droppings.

Now it's white, so white
it must repel water. And when you walk
down the hill to feed the ducks

they circle around the pond
following the beacon of your hair.
Shy mallards. Muscovies, domestic and ugly.

But it's the large whites you seem to cherish:
fragile, always sitting. Unlike the others, the ducks,
the days, they don't very often fly away.

Moving Away

Our life fits inside itself like a telescope.
At one end, looking
much smaller than it is, that other
packing: not only shirts
but the days we wore them, songs still
whirling above the phonograph
and some part of our eyes trapped in
the space between sash and stormwindow:
all the things we looked for. The edges of
ourselves like a deck
of cards, its regular jewels and familiar faces.
We could use them, toss them
precisely against the bases of the bare walls.
Or we could slide them out of the pack
and, carefully, from scratch,
build the old ones around us again.

The Yellow Poplar

Under its western edge a road curls
around and east. It is a pioneer tree:
the westernmost lead of an eastern species.
So close to where it is not, it is
almost something else: a quiet dark cousin,
a brother in the merchant marine. Under the road
soil changes. The other side
is wilderness. There is no place farther away.

Each year wind sings adventure, leaves
scatter west and stay like tracks on soft new earth.
Samara whirl off after the sun. At night
the roots dream, flex against the road's rough
belly, squeezing a slow, imperceptible crack.

In the deepest forest, far in
the East three centuries before, a colonist felled
trees westward. He could extend
the crowns like his own arms and eyes. And what
was touched was tamed.

April: spring limbs are blossomed heavy,
the yellow poplar puts its best
face far over the road. And I help,
following, leaning, rooted to my dead feet, my dying
legs. We are planning expeditions,
destinations. We are ready to move at any time
any way we can.

The Midwest

Desolation rich as topsoil.
This plain, flat-chested wife
bears children who are all body:
the farmer is a fist
sprinkling wolfsbane, charmed bones;
a young girl shaped like a forearm
holds the future
with bone thighs
and the ability to cook.

Out of the bankruptcy
comes the richness: whole fields
of corn and wheat
march off to the city
while the country sinks farther
into the flatness.
And lurching bright out of the rattle
of dark furrows, a geranium,
stem thick and gnarled
as an old woman's finger
pushing down a seed.
She is pregnant again, staggering
under the simple, breathing
dead weight.

Survival
for B.B.

A stringer of crappie and cats: all we could
ask of then and there. But in the shallows
deadwash churned with swarms of carp.
We dreamed ourselves starving, hunger
unrolling in us like a new moon. And you knelt
past shore slow as an oak, posed still
as the water they roiled: I believed it.

You touched their thin silver spines, stroked
the perfect fins. That much was easy. And
maybe that's the way a dream works. One carp wiggles
away, the lake goes quiet. We weren't
hungry enough, even though the cats and crappie were
shrinking, the raspberry bushes bare.

We took less than we could carry. It was all
we needed that day.

Falling

The plums have begun their gradual rot,
making a bog of the backyard.
Birds, drunk with decay
in their beaks,
thump against the wall
like men falling in their sleep.

A beetle leaves a plum hollow—
the bruised skin holding its place.
The sleeper never lands
but wakes in the empty pocket of the bed
feeling around for his life
like small change.

The Quilter

All these years making sense of rags,
ragged edges
of other lives, and I have saved only one,
to bury, Husband, with you.
It is a pattern I call *Blue Maze*:
you might use it as a map.

It carries our story, our shapes, two
decades of shirts off our backs.
How many nights
it hid winter. I could not
trust it to other hands, other
bodies. What love
it might feel that was not ours.

Take it with you then, two
layers and the air between,
stitched by my hand.
Thread runs through like a memory, on
both sides, *Blue Maze*, a puzzle of
show for the world, and next to you
the pure white that is ours, private.

Lull

Wind piled husks at the door
and made us sleepy.
Sacks of onion hung from the cellar
beams like scrota, and swayed—
or stood still while we did. Two
miles east an oak was impaled by
a broomstick. In the west, houses gave
in to vacuum, the river rippled
slightly and catfish
studied the intricacies of rafters.

In the sifting yellow lamplight, a few
of us kept aloft some
desiccated cornsilk, a game
for the lull between thunderclaps, moments
before and after the only two hymns
we all knew by heart. And the wind droned on,
filling the air with crescendo, with
an organ's thousand throats.

The Milking

She kicked. Some good
reason, or none: a tick on her flank
or just his cold hands on her teat.
But down he went, backwards, off
the stool and into the puddle,
spreading slow,
of muddy milk.
Then he was up, dripping and pounding,
his fists thudding bone
and she, chewing, doing the same
dance she'd do against flies.
We stayed back and laughed to ourselves:
it was comical. But he began
to concentrate, grabbed a long-handled spade
and as it swung through the still barn
air it made a *whoosh* like a scythe
and rang when it hit
as if he'd struck a stone half-submerged
in a garden. Now she hurt,
and tugged at her tether, bellowed. Soon
all the cows were crying and the spade kept
making that same *whoosh* and *clang*.
When blood began to smear
around her snout, we went outside,
leaned against the truck
and waited. Dust churned and
swirled in the dark doorway, slowed,
floated out in the thick August
heat and sank. When the bawling stopped

he came out, passed us, and into the house.
There was little damage: spilled milk,
she staring into her stall, blood
drying, caked on her muzzle.
And the spade in the middle of the floor,
the handle broken. It was a good
spade, the heaviest we'd ever lifted. The handle
was aged oak.
We didn't think it could ever break.

Building a Shack

No one builds a shack says my friend.
But we go ahead, in the architecture of scavenged
two-by-fours, the style of nothing but time.

I take the north and west walls,
he the south and east.
That's the most congenial division:

the diagonal. The beveled wedges
of souls coming together
like fine mitred veneer.

And this is where we come,
each to his corner-and-two-halves,
to make up these poems,

to leave and return
like seasons come round for nothing
except to weather the bare wood.

December: *American Bottoms* Farm

Wind is a whisper you can't make out:
the arm leaving the sleeve,
a fly's hiss fading in the ear of a cow.
The mind hollows out, listening.
Sleep settles over the eyes of the day
like a snow sheet.

Winter of silence,
when sound spends a holiday in the south,
when voices lie in brittle drifts.

A bell rings in another county,
faint, as if someone has died.
Old cornfields sink into themselves
and the wind buzzes:
a hawk brushing his wings against air,
the nostrils setting free a last breath.

Watching from the Footbridge

Heads thrown back, throats perpendicular
to shoesoles, two children laugh
and spin themselves into piles of loose elbows.

They think of themselves as saucers
wobbling on a tabletop,
the last draught of bathwater
caught in the drain. Their mother
thinks of brain damage,
one of them throwing up in the car.

Watching from the footbridge
over the slow creek,
she feels herself drifting,
her balance gone and nothing to hold onto.

In the Great Bear
Flathead Range, August 1976

At the excavation for marmots, on the lip
of a saucer bowled out by claws as long as
your outstretched hand, you crouch
low and quiet, the rodent's posture, and sight
two dark lanes through dewy meadow
grass: yours and his, splitting ninety acres
and spinning a dish of dirt
like a pendant on its chain. He left
the way he came, and but for minutes
you walked a collision course.

The digging came to nothing, and now
he is gone where you're headed, over the near rise
or the far mountain, asleep, burping
a fill of lilies. Or filled
with an emptiness like the one he just dug,
paused in the blind of lodgepole,
forelegs shaggy with dew and mud, claws

tipped and shiny. He waits upwind, always
prepared for surprise. But that is
the low view on high places. Stand up
and the air goes clear of his summer musk.
Shake off the marmot's small cautions,
that intricate network of tunnels, and walk on,
with him, behind him, singing loudly
and only to yourself.

Ursa Major

Trapper Peak, September 1975

On your back in juniper, a skeletal bear
grows above, a dipper full of dream
some mauled Indian spotted
centuries ago. Astronomers draw lines,
circle the dots with full-tailed bearish
shells as crude and empty as cookiecutters.

Here, you watch the starry bones grow
a body. In this place of pure dark,
constellations and nebulae too dim
in the city beam a silver-tipped coat,
and now and then some
distant sun flashes like a fang.

Homage to the Lost Pigeon

Where is the blind duty that sees
you home? Bearings taken in
the heart, blood's astrolabe, circling
in the updrafts,
careful miles over the earth's every curve.

There are points of reference, benchmarks
and black keys. Move through them
like blood through the torso, aiming
for the brain. Follow any pull:
hope, the draw of magnetic north,

or the moon,
shining somewhere on the one perfect spot.

The Distant Touch of Hands
for D & C

You that I'm glad to be alive with:
fingers in a closed hand,
at the grip of which the mingled
moistures of our lives flow over themselves
and never begin to dry.

Mornings on the way to work I cross
a creek that never flows down
your side of the country. Still,
I can be thankful: that I come out of my house,
survey the vanished fringes of my life
and wonder how they got out of reach,

on the same morning, in the same year as you;
thankful that just before we lapse and postpone
each other, we touch a handle or a tree
and those nerves that sleep between us tingle.

Steps

for Philip, age one

From the tips of my outstretched
arms to my neck
is four. In the time
it takes, one drop of blood loops
through my each careful finger.
And stops:
because I will it, because
he won't,
but leans into his second year, into
his steps
as though the center of gravity were
my heart. I stop it, too.
To slow down this walk we're on, this
learning of ropes. To put off that
one longest step into balance,
where even this is a kind of letting go.

Slides

The Photographs

So many of us smiling, waving. We were
happy to be there, glad
to leave. Or, knowing where
the camera leads, perhaps we wave at ourselves,
home again, smiling
at where we were, dreaming.

In the stillness of the print
we hold our breath, as though we were poised
for a race, moving always toward
some other place,
a smile's backdrop, from which we could
endlessly wave, endlessly outward.

Slides

I
for K & K, 1975

We always repose, try to rewind
the thin life caught in a shutter.
Another loss: we do little
damage: a nick in time.
Here we are, four of us standing by
McDonald Creek like respondents in a roll
call. The camera's timer
was a drumroll that went on too long.
Notice how my lips are
swan-diving out of a smile.
I could have lost a little weight then
and behind those beer-drunk eyes
are plans for running miles
I'm still planning. Such moves
are hard to make now. We're used to
the miles between us, the way
mountains tighten horizons. Up north,
the road alongside the creek will be locked
in snow another two months.

II
Carlton Lake, Bitterroot Range, 1976

The skid of moonrise
bobbing on a mountain lake, with a row
of thin hexagons sloping from corner to corner
like a molecular equation. They are mistakes,
flaws, blindnesses of the mechanical eye.

A pupil tunes itself to moonlight.
The diaphragm squints, peeling back
brightness, turning it loose
in the slow tunnel of the lens.
The moon and the water, all that light
carries and the light too.

But there is no moon here, no lake
collecting its tracks. This is what the camera
saw. It saw light. It saw itself
looking, and not looking,
without turning away.

III
Night baseball: St. Louis, 1970

A half–minute time exposure from the roof
of a parking garage into the stadium.
A player walked to the plate, took his practice
swings and stroked the first pitch
into the bleachers. His home run
locked now in a knot, all of it:
dream between dugout and batters' box,
impact, the touch of four bases.
Thirty seconds smacked onto paper like a bloodstain.
But it's all a blur, the victory, the glory.
His name's a red streak on the base
paths. The number looks like nothing Arabic.
You can't make out his face: it could have been
a first homer, a last, one of
a long string of lost balls . . .
Maybe he's lost too, adjusting his TV
in Jefferson City, thinking of the whack wood makes
on a baseball, wishing someone had taken
a picture. He'd go over it with a good eye,
measure the futile leap of the outfielder, search
the crowd for his one true fan: the man
who didn't cheer, but stayed calm, clearly in focus
until everything was over.

IV
November 20, 1976

The doctor says the baby may be too
big, rooted against the bedrock
of the pelvis and growing outward.
In the deep sights of the stirrups,
the pointed, clinical light, it may look
that way. But here is evidence:
you are between stairs, your large belly
plays maypole to the spine. The two
of you arc above floor boards,
suspended in solution like the bubble
of mid-air caught in an ice cube,
and holding the staircase delicately down.

V

W.H.W., 1969

Composition was easy: L-shaped.
Deceptive forward thrust of the wheelchair
and the man in it. The mirror
images of a hat's bill, a pipe.
The feet, off parallel, repeated themselves.
And in the unused corner, blur. The irony
of depth of field. Everything back there
is perfectly still, but it gets away.
We can't even look two places at once.
And always it's the near
that seems important. A second after
the shutter clicked a young man crossed
that empty space after a basketball.
He died in Asia two years later.
When I focused, my eye settled near center:
a right hand curled over the armrest. The left
was farther back, soft,
the wrinkles unclear, a gold ring
blazing below the knuckles, shrieking its
initial. But all that came out
was the right hand, the calluses.
Those fingers hooked around
the framework, not part of a grip,
but simple, pulled down by gravity.

VI
Close-up: 1973

We call it overexposure, the light
of inventories, interrogations. Under it
a leaf is a fraction of a plant. No more.
These are fingertips, drawn up
by a day in dishwater. Or the knuckles
of an unclaimed body that beached on a sandbar,
dead, say the newspapers, of exposure.
Flesh gets warped by the mad
tides of the scrub, the moon always
drags the river for dead.
And the sun moves over highwater. It happens
that quietly, covertly. A man gone
in for a wade gets bleached and bloated.
The soft pads of someone's pink
fingers hesitate too long under the sun
and the eyes pronounce them dead.

The Sinking of Clay City

for

William H. Wrigley
1890–1970

December 24, 1970

Finally, the great lode of arteries
has turned diamond and ice. Your life
in glass, mined by catheters,
the veins broken. Yesterday, two nights
before Christmas, we wheeled your chair
all through the hospital. *Lotsa
darkies in here*, you mumbled,
toothless, to the black nurse.
And three of us, wife, son, grandson,
collide in a race for deafness.
Today is not legendary. Snow
all afternoon leaves the ground
a sprung quilt, just the soft pad
and a jagged overhang on the windowsills.
The wind is white as pipesmoke, easy
to get lost in, to think ourselves elsewhere.
Today was all, brawler, cop,
coal miner, custodian. Corpse.
Accordion player. Perpetual finder of lost
dollars. Dead man: I turn
a better ear to your collapsed life.
I dig where before I pushed
aside snow, warm at the core,
too quick to live in your silence,
too deaf to hear through smoke.

Future

The black dome stays around us.
We walk toward the crepe of its walls,
an international dateline,
but days bleed into one
another, the tunnel always ahead.

To the man afloat on six children
the bell on a coal car rings like a buoy.
Years later, spread on the spit
of time payments, he straddles
his future: one leg up on tomorrow,

the other dragging behind.

Miners Shaking Hands with a Union Man
from a photograph

These men are solemn and strong,
their lungs black and bituminous.
Behind the photographer, Peabody's goons.

The woman, half-visible on the fringe
of the vignette, feels that way:
her husband vanished in the dark snow of a cave in.

And closely, through the heavy grain,
you can see they are armed.
The blunt handle of a shovel curled

in an arm's crook, a chain
wrapped around a fist
like a large and fraternal ring.

This is a show of force: it is not
important that the pale-skinned Peabody men
sweat around the butts of revolvers,

but that they know for once
the isolation of the mines,
the impenetrable blackness off camera.

Harmony

Blind Charley Bass said the whole world was
coal. The fire that took his eyes
left everything black, but after
the years had settled down his vague lids,
darkness turned white and detailed as lace, a light
by which he could see what he'd only heard before.
He taught himself accordion, to pick out
names in a crowd of steps, the
indelible signature of a sigh. On Friday nights
the crowd gathered in his living room.
From Bunker Hill and Lumaghi, from Hardscrabble:
One-Eyed Schmitt, Big Tits Molnar and Rooshun
Tony. Little Jim, Three-Toe Walker
and Fat: they moved aside the table, leaned
against the doorway, barbershopping.
They moved the widow Bass' picture and sat
on the washstand. And sang.
Five hours the coarse breath roared for life
and Charley's wheezy accordion rang clear
as clanged steel. At midnight, they shuffled out,
the swirl of their harmonies floating down dust,
like so many fine doilies,
covering the room with song.

Diary of the Strike
May 21, 1939

Picket lines are for fingers and legs:
how thin they are, how easy they'd give
under axe handles.
                     At noon
The Union Rep comes with a bag of radishes
and rye bread. We give thanks
for our fortunes: Billy Carruthers ran
the length of Mascoutah, Illinois
with his ankle bones chiseled off
and two nickels ringing in his pocket:
he could have lost it all.

The strikebreakers, cleaning their teeth
near the pool hall, are rumored to spit-
shine their boots with miners' blood.

When my line duty's over I'll get
right home. Potatoes and cabbage for dinner
again, but who'd complain? The goons
slice their steaks with the same knives
that cut off noses and thumbs. Near dark
we're all thumbs: the placards shaking,
the alleys lit with shadows.
                              No one's afraid
really. Just hungry, looking forward to dinner,
walking quietly home.

The Herrin Massacre
June 22, 1922

Nurses are not allowed, for these scabs'
wounds will never heal. Small boys
piss on a bullet hole, pump the lead of their pockets
in a cut throat. A young mother
burps her baby and shuffles dust
over a blood puddle,
as if her toes were distant things
working the pile in a carpet.

The men are off collecting corn
and red beans, their strike-pay gone on bullets,
the bullets gone. And if tomorrow
they should enter the empty church,
it would only be to give thanks,
to speak in low tones for a change,
to pay another month's dues.

Oh Yeah, the Mine Talks

                              Secrets
ain't no part of it though, just good learnin'.
And you better pay attention. When them timbers
creak just so it means they're givin' up
and lettin' down—sorta like bones,
the way a knee pops a little too loud
one last time. You smack the roof
of the loadin' room a few times
with the handle of your shovel before steppin' in.
Coal up there's supposed to sound good,
thunka thunka like a ripe melon. If it don't,
if it sounds muddy or don't ring even a little,
she's gonna fall. Maybe right then.
You gotta move fast. Then
there's the sounds a miner can't hear.
Too high, a dog whistle, a train way outa town.
Watch: cause rats hear it. A little
hiss of gas comin' in. That's when you wish.
All that time cussin' them rats for stealin'
your sandwich, laughin' about the one
what stole Henry's false teeth, or them whiskers
drug across your ankles that made your bones go cold:
you wish they was all here. But those rats,
they gone. Crawled out through their holes.
And you ain't never leavin' yours.

Tommyknockers

"Little people who go through the mine
tapping at the timbering to make sure it's sound."
—*Wallace Stegner*

Gnomes, keep your ears to the walls
so mine can follow
your code. I know your music
like the pulse in my pillow,
though sometimes
in my dreams, I dream
you're only dancing.

From Lumaghi Mine

Dear Father,
            Eleven days without sunlight. We go in
in the black morning fog, work and come out
having missed it all. We begin to appreciate the dark.
Too bright outside: faces white
as carbide, the shrill discs of real dishes.
It takes two days to get used to peripheral vision
again, the head light without the lamp.
      We rest after loading each car.
In that silence the seeping gas trickles,
as if we fished an underground stream for hours
without hearing water. So pain comes too,
when the muscles are still.
      I write while the others sleep. By the light
of my headgear the pencil feels like a pickaxe.
The moon is my sun and the sculptures
on the mine walls shimmer into constellations.
I have learned how not to see.
      Sometimes I am shocked by the whiteness
of my cuticles, glowing out of the nails
like slivers from an eclipse. They bob across the page,
fireflies, men walking up a shaft with lit lamps.
And the worn shovels, the hands, hang alongside
the body, coal dust healed into the calluses.
They seem odd, astir in the milk of the bedclothes
like frail and discolored spoons.
      Father, we are all the same. Dust fills in
the oldest wrinkles, the deepest scars. You see,
I am blackening: grey knuckles,
ears silting over. My eyes
are black as anthracite. The sun could ignite them
and they would burn for days.

The Sinking of Clay City

When the last mine closed
and its timbers turned pliable as treesap,
the town began to tilt, to slide
back into its past like a wave.

Old men, caught by the musk
of seeping gas, arrived at the mainshafts
hours before dawn. Their soft hands
turned the air like handles on new picks.

Here and there a house split,
a cracked wishbone,
and another disappeared like crawlspace
behind a landslide.

So the townspeople descended the sloping entrances,
found them filled with a green
noxious water. Each drank a little
and forgot about the sun.

Some dug at rusted beercans
or poked at a drowned rat, more patient
than dedicated archaeologists,
and waited for their other lives to join them.

The Last Trees
for Clyde

They seem desperate in their loneliness.
Cement in the knotholes
like cold cream embedded
under earlobes, their leaves
heavy with a black mascara.
In the airy bulk of
their hairdos are nests and old kites,
like faded barrettes.

They have only themselves.
Sometimes on windy Friday nights
they dance with each other.

This tiny wood is a failed bar,
the corner of the dancehall
nearest the restrooms.
Here, a twisted mimosa wilts
toward fall, a pale ash
dreams of rigid cedar root.

Resignation

Inertia keeps us
going, the ease we always felt
in descent. Streets have lost their
destinations, and already grass has begun
to sprout across the last gated mainshafts.
There is nothing to do with these houses
except die in them. The coal is gone.
We accept it, like the apple gutted
by worms and rotting inside out,
like the spider, whose intricate web
is bound for collapse
with the silent, empty barn.

The Race

*"The coal is gone and the children
have nothing to say."*
—Stanley Plumly

Each day, when school is out,
the streets erupt in quiet. There are
fathers inside worrying
fingers around bottles, babies
plucked dozing from breasts
like ripened peaches a holler might bruise.
Behind the hill behind the school
two boys have a footrace around the dead
tipple, where the winner
whoops in silence
and the other almost holds his breath.

Song of the Trapped Miners

A miner sees in the dark: a trapped
miner sees beyond. After twelve
hours the cloud of oxygen
thins to a pale fog, and we stop
digging. After twenty hours the rocks
turn soft as black velvet, the
mattress of unconsciousness.
Twenty-four hours, thirty,
the prismed light works in: blues,
then green and reds pass
from the coal and coalesce. We can see,
through the long lens of the cave in,
the tears of our families, sweat
making canals on the necks
of our comrades, the owner's
fierce impatience. We can see
rescuers coming nearer and nearer
then retreating, their deep eyes
taking in the pit they've dug themselves into.
We see the crowd breaking up
and moving off, the town beginning to glow
with candles. And at dark, one time
for each of our two eyes, the churchbell
sends a shock through the violet air,
and all the world goes blur.

The Wives of Trapped Miners

In thick shoes, they huddle under the tarpaulin,
elbows burrowing from the sleeves of sweaters:
they are as young as they have ever been.

The eldest of them is the only one crying.
Her unreclaimable future settles around her like slag.
She has gotten used to the spice of coal dust
or the scent of gas from the hat behind the door.

One woman rubs her large belly and smiles.
She has noticed the enclosure of her family: the child
coiled in the womb and the husband in the mineshaft.

The wait has gone on for two days
and not all the wives are here. Some are home
practicing widowhood. Some are praying in the company
church. And others are dancing in the bright halls

of their dreams, where their husbands give them
waltz after waltz, and stride to the long tables for punch.
The wives swing into overstuffed chairs,

suddenly shocked at their white dresses,
the fronts of them smudged with a fine black soot.

Coroner's Report

I begin again. There is so much
relief, but it is geological, the whorls
and contours of the skin shaded, exaggerated,
as though all the body had been fingerprinted.
But here: left hand, ring finger bears
a pale, white scar beneath the wedding band,
slightly green, perhaps from sulphur, or impure gold.
The pupils are dilated. Often, after the instant
of death, the eyes go on reaching, glaring
into the backs of the lids.
Always, it is the same unraveling. Each man's life
a callus, the skin like cowhide, eyes
honed on a whetstone of darkness. And where
is the fat? There are only these lobes of bicep,
the taut cords of sinew and tendon. Inside, bones
have bent and gelled the color
of creosote, heavy and hard as ironwood.
In its jar, a miner's brain matches the grey
matter of the banker. The stomach has grown strong
gripping on itself, and the heart has learned
all possible rhythms: of pick and pulley,
of shovel, the crack of tie and timber. Somewhere,
loved ones are waiting for
explanations, a reprieve, some new reason for dying.
But this is all: these two hard pods of
breath, curse and cry caught in fossils.
These lungs, and thousands more, seeded on
the hillside like cumbersome, worthless rhinestones.

Legacy

for Jack Conroy

I am a tired man and getting
to be an old one. I know all the octaves
a mine's roof can chime: when it will fall.
And in certain lights I can see
in the eyes around me who it will fall on.

The pick hangs on my shoulder,
a crippled child I thought would stop growing.
So far three of my sons have
followed me into the mine. I am the fool
buffalo, first over the pishkun.

There is nothing in a contract for a coughing son
and all I have to pass on
is the wisdom of darkness, something
to bite on for pain. The elevator comes
down the shaft dried on one side by daylight.
Old miners read it like a sundial.

ROBERT WRIGLEY teaches at Lewis–Clark State College, Lewiston, Idaho. He lives in Clarkston, Washington with his wife, Vana and son, Philip.

THE SINKING OF CLAY CITY was designed at Copperhead by K West. 1000 copies are sewn in paper covers. A limited edition of 50 are bound in cloth over boards and signed by the poet. The type is 11 pt. Bembo, a copy of a roman cut by Francesco Griffo for the Venetian printer Aldus Manutius. First in Cardinal Bembo's *De Aetna* (1495), it was the forerunner of the standard European type of the next two centuries. Set by Irish Setter, Portland.

The illustration is by Tree Swenson.